POEM DEPOT

Aisles of Smiles

Poems and drawings by

Douglas Florian

DIAL BOOKS FOR YOUNG READERS *An imprint of Penguin Group (USA) LLC*

DIAL BOOKS FOR YOUNG READERS

PUBLISHED BY THE PENGUIN GROUP
Penguin Group (USA) LLC, 375 Hudson Street, New York, NY 10014
USA • Canada • UK • Ireland • Australia • New Zealand • India • South Africa • China
penguin.com

A PENGUIN RANDOM HOUSE COMPANY

Library of Congress Cataloging-in-Publication Data
Florian, Douglas.
[Poems. Selections] • Poem Depot : Aisles of Smiles / by Douglas Florian . • pages cm. • Audience: Ages: 9–11 • Audience: Grades: 4 to 6 • An illustrated collection of silly nonsense poems about topics kids care about: talents, avoiding homework, friends and more. Poems.
ISBN 978-0-8037-4042-6 (hardcover) • I. Title. • PS3556.L589P633   2014   811'.54—dc23

Printed in China
1 3 5 7 9 10 8 6 4 2

Book design by Sarah Creech • Type set in Naughties and Bookman Old Style
The publisher does not have any control over and does not assume any responsibility for author or third-party websites or their content.

For our children,
Naomi, Ariel, Raphael, Or, and Anael

.CONTENTS.

· AISLE 1 ·
Wit & Whimsy

Welcome

Welcome to Poem Depot,
With smiles in the aisles.
There's laughs galore
Inside this store,
And fun that runs for miles.
The poems in here
Are full of cheer,
With whimsy and with wit.
You'll laugh so much
At jokes and such,
Your sides will surely split.
Welcome to Poem Depot—
Relax and stay a while.
When you walk in
You'll surely grin,
And leave wearing a smile.

Rooster

The rooster crowed this morning,
Its comb a brilliant red.
The rooster crowed this morning,
And then went back to bed.

A Friend

A friend is a friend,
A friend to the end.
She's loyal and faithful and true.
A friend's always there
To help and to care.
She's honest and always true blue.
And when you're in need,
She'll come with great speed.
If need be she'll yell and she'll holler.
A friend is a friend,
A friend to the end.
So friend,
Can you loan me a dollar?

Honee

Insect Asides

Some ladybugs are really men.
And crickets don't play cricket.
Though they cavort, they don't play sport
On lawns or in a thicket.
A dragonfly is not a fly.
It's not a dragon either.
No butter on a butterfly,
And bees cannot spell neither.
A centipede has not one cent.
A weevil does not weave.
And if you don't stop bugging me,
Then I'll ask you to leave!

4

Book Report

The worst book of all
That I've ever read
Annoyed me so much that
I fell out of bed.
It gave me a headache
And made me throw up.
It was a disaster,
a failure,
a flop.
My palms started sweating.
My poor heart would race.
And forty-three times I found
I'd lost my place.
It rumbled my stomach.
It rattled my brain.
And surely tomorrow
I'll read it again.

A Bicycle Built for Forty-Eight

A bicycle built for forty-eight:
The first person's early.
The last person's late.

Easy Reader

Monday I read a newspaper.
Tuesday a magazine.
Wednesday just one article
About a Danish queen.
Thursday six short stories.
Friday four long plays.
This weekend I will stay at home,
Read people's palms all day.

Food Play

I play football with a melon.

I play baseball with a pear.

I play Frisbee with a pancake

As I toss it through the air.

I play Ping-Pong with some soup nuts.

I play tennis with my dinner.

And though I'm told "Don't play with food,"

At least I'm getting thinner.

Poem Home

I started to sit,
To sit in a chair.
Then suddenly realized,
The chair was not there.
I started to climb,
To climb up the stair.
Then suddenly realized,
The stair was not there.
I started to write,
To write down this poem.
Then suddenly realized,
I'd left it at home.
I'd left it at home on a chair by the stair.
But the chair, and the stair, and the poem were not there.

Driven

Sometimes I race a bicycle.
Sometimes I drive a car.
Sometimes I ride a railroad train
And travel very far.
Sometimes I drive a motorbike.
But when I'm feeling lazy,
I stay at home
And write a poem
And **drive** my mother crazy.

Scared

I'm scared of wild animals:
Of lions, tigers, bears.
I'm scared of climbing mountains,
Or falling off of chairs.
I'm mortified of monsters,
Or each and every ghost.
Next Thursday is a science test—
And that scares me the most.

More

I want more jokes.
I want more fun.
I want more candy
By the ton.
I want more laughs.
I want more smiles.
I want more cookies,
Piles and piles.
I want more games.
I want more friends.
I want my more
To never end.

Eaten Path

I ate six sizzling hot dogs.
Four hamburgers I grilled.
Five bags of roasted peanuts.
Two quarts of grape juice, chilled.
I ate a crate of oranges,
Including every pit.
I ate so very much today,
My stomach yelled, "I quit!"

Train to Nowhere

We're taking a train to nowhere.
We're boarding at never o'clock.
We packed up our bags full of nothing:
No shirts and no skirts and no socks.
There's nowhere that we aren't going.
There's no place that we will not pass.
We're taking a train to nowhere—
And we're going nowhere fast.

·AISLE 2·
Chortles & Chuckles

One of Those Days

Have you ever had one of those days

Where you seem to be lost in a puzzle or maze?

Where you can't find your nose and you're missing your ears?

Have you ever had one of those years?

Pink Purse

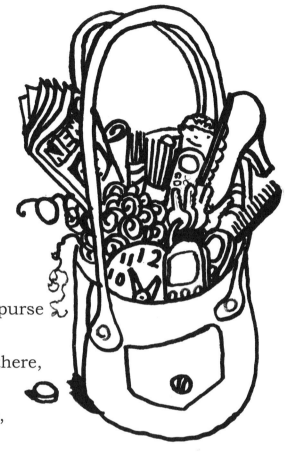

My mother has a bright pink purse
That's very very big.
She keeps all of her makeup there,
As well as her red wig.
She put a pair of socks inside,
As well as high-heeled shoes.
There's magazines and books in there,
Some six from which to choose.
She stows some extra underwear,
A new Swiss army knife,
Her all-time favorite good-luck charm
That she's had most her life.
She loves to stash all of her cash
And though it may sound silly—
Inside that bright pink purse of hers
She keeps my brother, Billy.

Exercise

First I did ten push-ups.
Then I did six squats.
Afterwards some nothings—
Lots, and lots, and lots.

Appetite

Today I have no appetite.
I do not wish a single bite
Of any food or any drink.
There's nothing that I'd like, I think.
I do not wish a meal of fish,
Nor sirloin steak upon a dish.
I do not want to eat French fries,
Or pretzel sticks or pizza pies.
I've got no yen for any eggs,
Or turkey breast or chicken legs.
Don't serve me broccoli or peas,
And please don't give me any cheese.
For soup or salad I don't care—

What's that you say? Candy today?
I'm hungry as a bear!

My Closet

Don't dare go in my closet—
For it's an awful mess.
I'm terrified
To go inside
Each time I have to dress.
The shirts are mostly inside-out,
The pants strewn on the floor.
So many sweaters pile up,
You cannot close the door.
My shabby shoes
Were on the news
For stinking to high heaven.
My underwear
Is known to scare
My cousins Kyle and Kevin.
My cowboy hat
Is squished quite flat
From all the junk in there:
Like fishing poles and hockey goals
And Grandma's rocking chair.
Great ghosts and goblins haunt the place,
Six crickets and a mouse.
There's only one solution:
It's time to sell the house!

I Hate Broccoli

I hate broccoli.
I hate peas.
I hate liver
And Swiss cheese.
I hate milk
And I hate bread.
I hate lettuce—
Every head.
I hate green beans,
Short or long.

I love French fries
All day long.

Good

Dave is good at diving.
Ronnie likes to run.
Pam excels at Ping-Pong.
Gil thinks golf is fun.
Tina's good at tennis,
Ben at basketball.

Little Nell does very well
At doing nothing at all.

Test Dive

Dave took a dive.
(Dave weighs a lot.)
Dave's in the pool.
The water is not.

Lazy

I didn't read a book today.
I didn't take a hike.
I didn't shoot a basketball.
I didn't ride my bike.
I didn't sweep the floor today,
Or bake a loaf of bread.
And all because
And all because
I didn't get out of bed.

Slippery Sam

They call me Slippery,
Slippery Sam
'Cause nobody knows
Just where I am.
I slip inside a room with ease,
And just as quick
Leave if I please.
I slide through cracks;
I crawl 'neath doors.
I've even slipped
Between two floors.
I'm Slippery Sam.
I am so thin
That I can slide
Right outta my skin.

House Pets

We have six dogs and seven cats,
Three gerbils and a dozen bats,
Two turtles and five chimpanzees,
Nine nanny goats with knobby knees,
Ten elephants and one gray mouse.

I think we need a bigger house.

Swiss Navy Knife

It has a knife
To save your life.
A pen and pencil, too.
It clips your nails,
Opens your mail,
And squeezes paper glue.
It tells your weight.
It cleans your plate.
Tells time with great precision.
It sings a tune
All afternoon.
And it does long division.
It takes out corks.
It has four forks,
A spoon to ladle gravy.
But one thing's wrong—
For all along—
There isn't a Swiss navy.

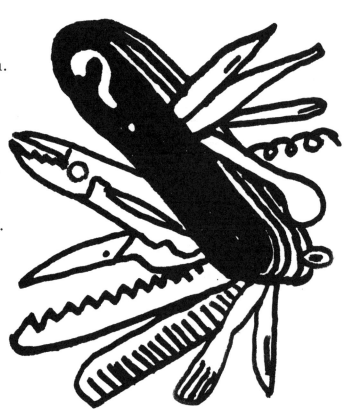

Crazy Cozy

On this cold and wintry night
I tucked myself in bed real tight,
Beneath a bright red flannel sheet
Designed to warm the coldest feet.
I've got four blankets made of wool;
My pillow with goose down is full.
Beneath it all I'm tucked in tight,
But I forgot to close the light!

Bad Boys and Grisly Girls

Micky likes to pick his nose.

Inky has ten stinky toes.

Hester pesters both her sisters.

Buster loves to puncture blisters.

Nelly never trims her nails.

Telly eats from garbage pails.

Billy bullies all the girls.

Willy steals his mother's pearls.

Stacy's good at crazy faces.

Tracy always changes places.

Worst of all is lovely Dove.

Dove does *all of the above.*

Foot Notes

I have six pairs of sandals
And sixty pairs of shoes,
In all assorted colors
And varieties of hues.
I like to wear my rubber boots—
Splash puddles in the street.
But best of all,
Since I was small,
I walk in my bare feet.

.AISLE 3.
Funny Bones & Belly Laughs

Po m

Th s po m is mis ing le ters.
It's mis ing q ite a f w.
Wh re th y did go
I do n t kno .
I do n t kno .
Do y u?

Room Doom

My mother said to clean my room
And then to sweep the floor.
I'm in a funk . . .
There's so much junk . . .
I can't get in the door.

Froggly

They say that if
You kiss a frog,
It turns into a prince.
But when I kissed a frog it changed
Into my cousin Vince.

Mean Meat Loaf

Mother made us meat loaf.
Meat loaf made for five.
When it turned black,
We took it back
And buried it alive.

Genie Chair

Some people sit on sofas.
Some much prefer a chair.
But genies are quite special—
They sit on top of air.

Cloudless

There's not a single cloud today
Across the whole wide nation.
But there is rain in sunny Spain,
Where clouds are on vacation.

Big Den

Our living room's for living.
Our dining room's to dine.
But in our den,
Now and again,
We keep a lovely lion.

Old Mother Hubbard

Old Mother Hubbard
Went to the cupboard
To fetch her poor dog a bone.
But when she got there
The cupboard was bare.
She ordered Chinese on the phone.

35

Drift

Mary had a little lamb,
Whose fleece was white as snow;
So Mary took her snowplow
Wherever they would go.

Pease Plan

Pease porridge hot,
Pease porridge cold,
Pease porridge in the pot,
Nine days old.
Some like it hot.
Some like it cold.
I'll pass on the Pease porridge
Nine days old.

The Old Woman in the Shoe

There was an old woman
Who lived in a shoe.
She had so many children
She didn't know what to do.
So she hired nine nannies
With one wondrous maid,
And now she relaxes
Outside in the shade.

No Mow

My father said to mow the lawn—
I mowed it in two hours.
When I was done, to have some fun,
I mowed all of the flowers.
I mowed the bushes and the shrubs,
Our little apple tree.
I mowed the hedge flat as a ledge—
Now stumps are all you see.
The leprechaun upon the lawn,
I clipped down to his toes.
And I made green confetti from
Our big green garden hose.
I mowed the fence—
It made no sense—
The signposts on our lane.
I don't think Father ever will
Ask me to mow again.

Us Bus

There're 99 people inside of this bus
With 99 more on the top.
    And all this is fine—
    As we roll down the line,
As long as the bus doesn't stop.

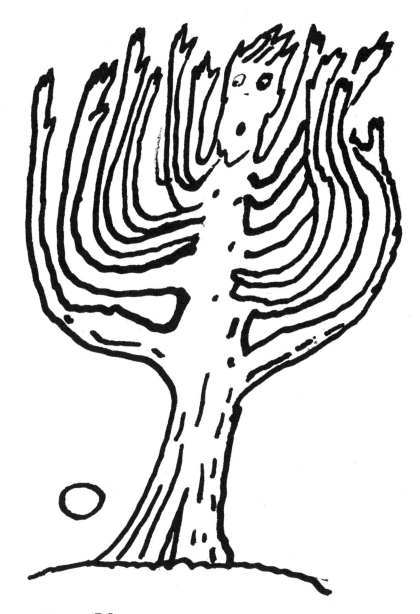

Tree Wear

The summer trees are dressed in green.

In autumn, gold and tangerine.

The winter trees are naked, nude—

No clothes at all, how very rude!

Lost Appetite

One day I lost my appetite,
So I commenced to look
In every nook and cranny,
In every box and book.
Inside my vest, my bedroom chest,
Beneath my wicker chair.
How I did hunt from back to front;
It simply wasn't there.
I tried all day in every way
To search and scan and dig.
But after all that looking
I was hungry as a pig.

Mr. John Ember

Mr. John Ember
Doesn't remember
If it's November
Or if it's December.
Or even the Fall
He cannot recall.
He keeps a small note
By the side of his bed,
Reminding him that
He should screw on his head.

Tall Tale

They questioned Abe Lincoln,
Who stood six foot three,
How tall is the right height
A person should be.
Abe Lincoln responded
"There's one rule I've found:
A man should be so tall,
His feet reach the ground."

Eggs

Eggs are egg-cellent.
Eggs are great
In a bowl or on a plate.
Sunny-side up or
Sunny-side down,
With green onions
Or hash browns.
Poached or scrambled,
Boiled or fried,
Eat your eggs raw—
Open wide!

Dawn's Yawn

Dawn opened her mouth
With such a great Y
                      A
                       A
                      A
                   W
                 N

She swallowed herself
And now she is gone.

Seasonings

How would you like some seasoning,
Some seasoning on your dish?
Some ginger in your salad
Or paprika on your fish?
And do you take some salt in soup?
Perhaps some pepper, too?
Or will you have some nothing?
Does nothing work for you?

Alien Sweater

I'm knitting a brand-new wool sweater.
It's for my new alien friend.
She's got forty arms, my friend Yetta,
I fear that I never will end.

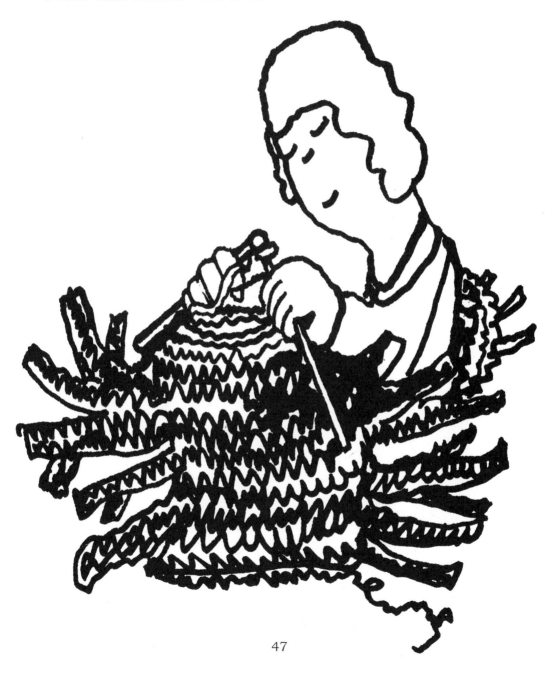

Hair

Brown
Or blond
Or black as can be.
My dad's is gray,
But that's thanks to me.

Soup of the Day

I wanted to cook some savory soup,
But didn't have any potatoes,
Or carrots or peas,
Or chicken or cheese,
Or meat or a beet,
Or tomatoes.
I didn't have rice
Or noodles or spice.
No beans and no greens
And no squashes.
So I told my daughter
To boil some water
And throw in some rubber galoshes.

Half-Empty Glass

Some say the glass is half empty.
Some say it's half full instead.
But after I drank all the water,
I burped, and I went to bed.

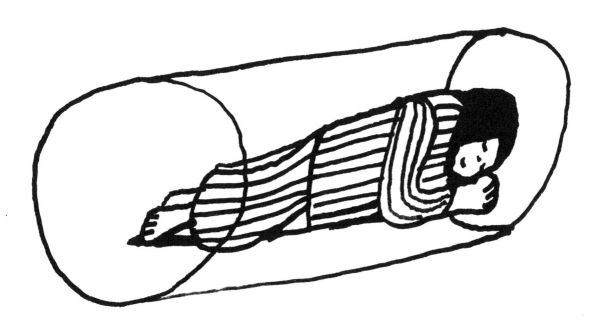

Favorite Shirt

My favorite shirt
Is so full of dirt.
What's worse it's well worn
And tattered and torn.
It's twice overrun.
Should really be done.
But it's what I wore
When I hit my home run.

Water Water

Water, water everywhere
But not a drop to drink.
I've watched water rise
Clear up to my eyes.
Will somebody unclog my sink?!

A Monster Is Hiding

A monster hides
Beneath my big bed,
With eight green eyes
Upon its head.
It's ghastly, and gruesome,
And ghoulish, and gory.
And that's why each night
I must read it a story.

What a Monster Ate

It ate candy.
It ate cake.
It ate Kansas,
By mistake!

School Fool

History's a mystery.
Math is just a bore.
Science class I'll never pass.
Music makes me snore.
Chemistry is difficult.
Gym I sleep all day.
But when it's lunch,
I have a hunch
I'll always get an A.

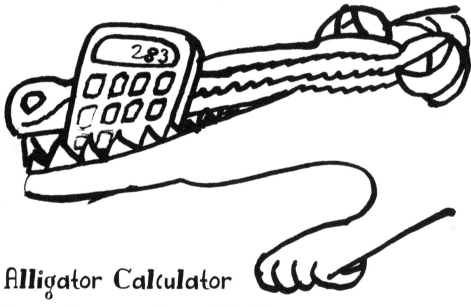

Alligator Calculator

I wanted to count the teeth inside
The mouth of an alligator.
I reached 23,
Then he swallowed me.
I'll have to finish later.

I'm So Hungry

I'm so hungry I could eat a horse,
And a moose, with a goose next course.
I'm so hungry I could eat Kentucky
And Rhode Island, Vermont, if I'm lucky.
I could eat the Earth with ease—
Except, of course, the peas, please.

Erase Her

I made a mistake,
For goodness sake,
While writing on a test.
So I erased, with greatest haste,
That itty-bitty pest.
Erased the paper and my desk,
Erased the walls and door.
Erased my teacher, bit by bit.
Don't need this eraser no more.

Snow Way

Snow up to my ankles.
Snow up to my knees.
Snow up to my shoulders.
Come dig me out now, please!

Deep Sleep

I went to sleep,
A sleep so deep,
I slept for sixty years.
And when I woke,
The bed had broke,
And weeds grew from my ears.
I rubbed my eyes,
I swatted flies,
And scratched my scraggly head.
I blew my nose,
Wiggled my toes,
And then went back to bed.

Hair Scare

I tried to comb my hair today.
My hair swallowed the comb.
There's several creatures in my hair
That call my hair their home.
My hair is quite unruly.
It's truly very wild.
And it treats me so cruelly
Since I was a small child.
It makes a squeaky noise
When teacher passes by
That scares all of the boys
And makes the girls all cry.
Each time I get a haircut,
My hair swallows the scissors.
And if you run your hand through it,
It may get caught in fissures.
I cannot wrap it in a cap,
No cowboy hat or bowler.
I need to stick my hair so thick
Beneath a big steamroller.
My friends today all stay away.
I hardly ever see 'em.
What's good is that my hair one day
Will go in a museum.

Imaginary Friend

I have an imaginary friend; we play
Almost every other day.
We fish for sunfish, hunt for frogs,
Look for creepy things in logs.
We catch grasshoppers,
Jump in lakes,
Spy on spiders,
Run from snakes.
But one day while we climbed a tree,
I thought: Maybe the imaginary friend
Is me!

This Chair

This chair is so comfy,
So perfectly plush,
I've no need to move,
And I'm not in a rush.
This chair removes cares,
All despairs, and all stress.
I'm making this chair
My new mailing address.

Wild Willy

Wild Willy wrestled bears,
Tackled tigers, and juggled hares.
Wild Willy out-chased cheetahs,
Carried elephants ninety-nine meters.
Wild Willy could heave up a house,
But Wild Willy was scared of a mouse.

Call a Head

They told me I should call a head
So call a head I did.
But now I'm stuck with my own head,
And this here head from Sid.
I solve math problems twice as fast,
Speak Russian, French, and Dutch.
But when I argue with myself
Then two heads are too much!

Rome and Room

Rome wasn't built
In just one day,
Or even in a year.
But just to clean
My messy room
May take much more,
I fear.

Nose Blows

There lived a man who blew his nose
So strong it blew off half his clothes.
He blew his nose so strong again,
He flew from France to southern Spain.
He blew it super-dupiter—
And found himself on Jupiter.

About Face

I woke up Monday morning
And went to wash my face,
Then noticed that my nose and mouth
Were missing from their place.
Both of my ears had disappeared.
Two toes were there instead.
I washed my face
So out of place
And went straight back to bed.

Haunted Home

I roamed into a haunted home,
A spooky kooky place.
Big bats were flying overhead;
One flew into my face.
Groans and moans and rattling bones
All filled the air with fear.
The creepy sound of creaking doors and
Windows I could hear.
The rooms were gloomy as a tomb,
With cobwebs everywhere.
And tentacles of creatures crept
From underneath the stair.
I roamed inside this haunted home,
But what scared me the most—
I looked inside a mirror and
I saw I was a ghost!

Climb Rhyme

I climbed a tree
One branch at a time,
Up to the top—
I love to climb.
And on the way
I saw a nest,
Three squirrels, then
I took a rest.
And when I reached
The top, the crown,
I wondered how
Would I get down.

AISLE 6.
Tons of Puns

Where My Cat Sleeps

My cat sleeps
Beside a door,
On a table,
In a drawer,
Upon my phone,
Or on a chair,
Blocking my way
On a stair,
By a window,
On my head.
Everywhere

Except her bed.

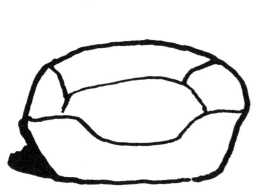

Down-Under Swimmer

I made a mistake,
A very big blunder:
I swam from Japan
To Australia—down under.
I'm **so** glad I made it,
And **I** didn't drown,
But my **down side** is upside
And **upside** is down.

In a Fog

Today my head is in a fog.
I'm neither here nor there.
I can't recall my middle name.
I fell right off my chair.
I tied my shoes on backward.
My shirt is inside out.
I ate my bowl of cereal
With juice and sauerkraut.
I put on my wool overcoat,
Though it's ninety degrees.
And wrapped my favorite scarf around
My ankles and my knees.
I went to walk the dog outside—
Instead the dog walked me.
And when I took the garbage out,
I put it up a tree.
I placed a dozen tulip bulbs
Inside of lightbulb sockets,
And tried to squeeze three bowling balls
Inside of my back pockets.
Today my head is in a fog.
A fog is in my head.
Until the weather's better there,
I'm going back to bed.

Talking Dog

I have a big bulldog named Billy.
He talks to me all night and day
About all the places he's been to
And just where he's hoping to stay.
He brags of his medals and trophies,
And all the awards that he's won.
He boasts of his girlfriend named Sophie,
And all the great deeds that he's done.
He says he once traveled to China
To dine with an emperor there.
And claims that in North Carolina
He's marshal of their big state fair.
I have a big talking dog Billy.
I'll sell him for five bucks to you.
For though he can talk himself silly,
Perhaps half his claims aren't true.

Fishy Wishbone Wish

I made a wishbone wish today
But didn't get my wish.
For though I won that wishbone wish,
I see I'm still a fish.

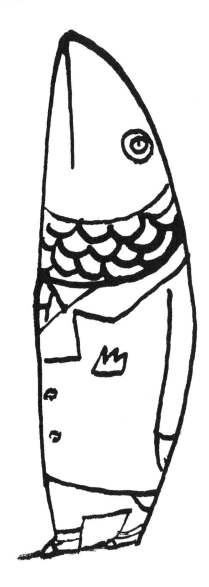

Marty's Magic Show

Marty showed us magic stunts,
Astonishing to see:
Pulled rabbits out of top hats,
From locks and chains broke free.
He hid five golf balls in his hand,
A cat inside his cape.
A lizard suddenly appeared
And balanced on a grape.
We'd really like to thank him now
For all the things he's done,
But right before our very eyes
He disappeared—he's gone!

Hate to Wait

I've been waiting in line
For some ten years or more,
And my hair has grown gray
And my feet are quite sore.
My backbone is frozen.
My knees are all stiff.
And I'm starting to feel
Like I fell off a cliff.
The line moves so s l o w l y ,
Like watching grass grow,
Or seeing paint dry, but even more slow.
I've waited here patiently
Some ten years or more,
But I can't remember
What this line is for.

Dramatic Attic

It's crowded in my attic
With junk piled into trunks.
There's broken plates
By crates and crates,
And rusty old bed bunks.
There's piles of files in boxes.
Old clothes fill chests of drawers.
There's records to the rafters.
Old china fills armoires.
I hated this stuffy attic,
So crowded I could shout.
But now that I am up here,
I'm stuck and can't get out!

Elephant's Skin

An elephant's skin is so saggy,
So rough and so wrinkly and baggy,
With lines like the tracks of a train.
But elephants never complain.

Not Myself

I'm really not myself today.
I think I'm someone other.
Perhaps I'm Thomas Jefferson,
Or Simple Simon's mother.
I'm really not myself today.
I think I'm someone new:
Like Dracula or Frankenstein,
Or what is worse—I'm you!

Mermaid

A mermaid is
Half woman, half fish.
Does she sleep on a bed,
Or else on a dish?

I Do Not Like

I do not like short people.
I'm not too fond of tall.
I rather hate all big folk,
Especially those small.
I steer clear of thin fellows
And portly persons, too.
I hate to face
The human race,
Except, of course, for you!

Ditty-Dum

Ten of my brothers are ditty.
Three of my brothers are dum.
Dum-ditty-ditty
Ditty-ditty-ditty-dum
Ditty-ditty-ditty-ditty
Ditty-dum!

Minotaur or Centaur

Half man–half horse
Is a minotaur.
Half horse–half man
Is centaur.
Or else the other way round.
I'm never really sure.

What Does?

What does a
Baga Baga
Dinga Donga do?
I'm not sure, but
There's one behind you!

·AISLE 7·
Jests & Jives

Shout Out

Leo let out
Such a stupendous shout
That his outsides are in
And his insides are out.

My Dog

My dog chased his tail around
Until one day he caught it.
He ate his tail and his whole self—
I should have never bought it.

Big Fish

The big fish eat the small fish.
The small fish eat the teensy.
The teensy eat the eensy-weensy
Eensy-weensy-weensy.

X-ray Day

They took an X-ray of my head,
And they found out, much to my dread,
That there was half a brain in there.
The rest was filled with just hot air.
I scratched my head, let out a cough.
I've **half a mind** to tell them off!

My Great-Great-Grandpapa

I asked my great-great-grandpapa,
"What hides inside your wrinkles?"
He said, "I keep my keys in there
And lots of periwinkles."

I asked my great-great-grandpapa,
"Why do you walk so slow?"
He answered me,
"So I can see
All things where I may go."

My Grandpapa's Car

My grandpapa once had a car
As old as grandpapa.
It went Grandpa! pa! pa! pa! pa!
Pa! pa! pa! pa! pa! pa!

How Do You Do?

I asked a man, "How do you do?"
He said, "How do you don't?"
I asked him, "Sir, what do you want?"
He said, "How will you won't?"
I questioned him, "What do you mean?"
"What mean you do?" he said.
Then I just ran home very fast
And jumped right into bed.

Rain Pain

Rain, rain—
Go away!
Come again another day,
Like March thirteenth,
Three thousand three.
Until then,
Please don't rain on me!

Mr. Carumba

Mr. Carumba is so very wide,

He takes up six seats when he goes for a ride.

For him it's a challenge to fit through a door.

He doesn't wear one belt, he wears twenty-four.

And just like a beach ball, he rolls down the stairs.

He's already broken one hundred five chairs.

When he walks on sidewalks he leaves behind cracks.

And seven course meals are for him merely snacks.

The shadow he casts sometimes covers two states.

He uses great satellite dishes as plates.

He wears a big circus tent for a top hat.

He eats with a pitchfork and drinks from a vat.

Nuts

There is no cash in cashews.
No peas in peanuts, too.
No cans are in a pecan.
So I say, "Nuts to you!"

Overdressed

I put on six sweaters,
Four coats, and what's more,
A dozen new scarves—
But can't get through the door.

Hold Your Horses!

They said, "Hold your horses!"
They told me to wait.
But horses are heavy,
And I'm running late!

Worse Weather

First rain.
Then snow.
Then hail.
Then sleet.
I'm glad I'm me
And not the street.

Pets

Bruce has ten pet roosters.
Ben has ten pet hens.
Fran has ten tarantulas,
But not too many friends.

.AISLE 8.
Rib-Ticklers & Sidesplitters

The Greatest Invention

The greatest invention was not the car,
Not the lightbulb and not the guitar,
Not the train and not the plane,
Not the umbrella, which blocks all the rain.
No, the greatest invention,
It may seem absurd,
The greatest invention by far is
The word.

Pet Dragon

I walk my big pet dragon.
I walk him twice a day.
Then spend ten hours cleaning up—
There's not much time to play.

Ambidextrous

Being ambidextrous is really rather sweet.
I write with left, I write with right,
And then write with my feet.

Frog Ugly

With warty skin and big bug eyes,
A frog won't win a beauty prize.
A frog's so ugly you could wince,
But kiss one once and he's a prince!

Mammoths

The mammoths were mammoth in size,
With mammoth tusks, and trunks, and thighs.
In mammoth size did mammoths grow.
But they lived mammoth years ago.

Time

You can't see time
Or taste
Or smell
Or talk to time,
But time will tell.

Four Eyes

Our teacher has eyes in the back of her head.

She's constantly watching her classes.

But we are not worried at all today.

Our teacher forgot her eyeglasses.

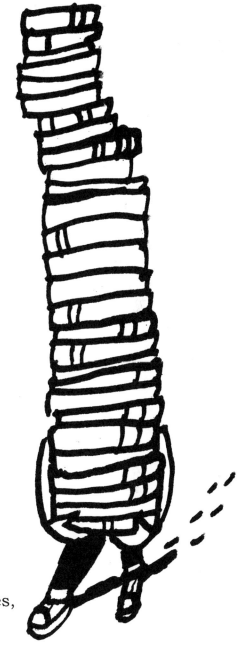

Billy Blaze

I'm Billy Blaze.
I wrote ten plays
And seven thousand poems,
Composed six hundred symphonies,
Designed eight hundred homes.
I've written fourteen thousand songs.
A million books I've sold.
But what's amazing most of all:
I'm only eight years old.

Baby Change

They told the magician,
"Change the baby, already!"
So he changed her into
Meatballs and spaghetti.

Cereal

A bowl of oatmeal.
A bowl of flakes.
A bowl of bowling balls—
We all make mistakes.

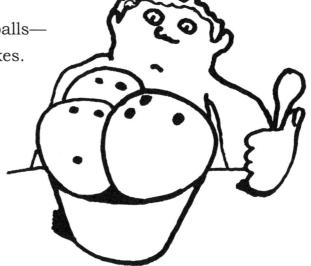

Walk Talk

I'm walking, walking, walking from New York to San Jose.
Each day I'm growing closer, growing closer every day.
There's one thing I should tell you
About this long great schlep—
Is that I'm walking backward,
Walking backward every step.

Webbed

I do not have a website,
Web e-mail, or web log.
But what I've got is four webbed feet
For I'm a worldwide frog.

My Favorite Color

My favorite color's not yellow or green.
Not red and not blue and not bright tangerine.
Not pink, and not olive, not purple, not plum.
My favorite color is chocolate. YUM!

I Am a Robot

I am a robot,
A robot I am.
I'm fully connected,
And my name is Sam.
I've got robot children
And one robot wife.
To dream robot schemes
Is the theme of my life.
I tried to join Facebook;
It's such a cool space.
But they kicked me off
For I don't
Have a
Face.

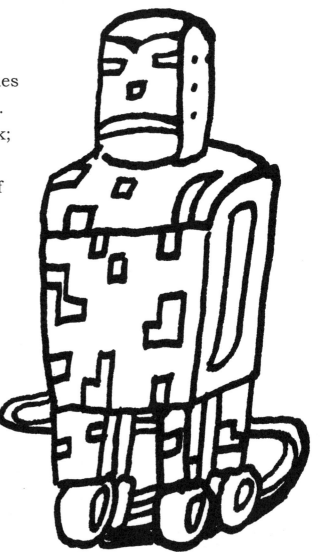

Big Bubble

I'm blowing up a bubble of
My favorite bubble gum.
My mother says it's stupid, and
My father says it's dumb.
I started last November,
And they tell me now it's May.
My bubble's getting bigger,
Getting bigger every day.
Yes it really is gigantic,
Some three hundred feet in girth.
But now I'm getting nervous
'Cause I'm ninety miles from Earth.

Small Change

My mother said that change is good.
I shouldn't stay the same.
So first I changed my underwear,
And then I changed my name.
I changed my friends.
I changed my school.
I changed my home address.
I changed my arms.
I changed my legs.
I changed into a mess.
I changed my bed.
I changed my head.
I changed my eyes to blue.
And though you may not realize it—
I just changed into YOU!

Love Potion

I mixed a love potion
Inside of my sink—
A crazy concoction,
Then started to drink.
It made me quite queasy
And gave me a fright.
Then I started kissing
All people in sight.
I kissed my four cousins
And my aunt Metilda,
My neighbor Eduardo
And his friend named Nilda.
I kissed a policeman,
Whose name was Attila,
But I didn't stop till
I kissed a gorilla.

· AISLE 9 ·
Jokes & Pokes & Funny Folks

Jugglers

Oren juggles oranges.
Perry juggles pears.
Anna juggles pineapples,
As many as she dares.
Sally juggles salad bowls.
Barry basketballs.
Jerry juggles jugglers.
Let's hope that no one falls.

The Computers Are Down

The computers are down.
The computers are down.
The power has turned off
Throughout the whole town.
The cars all stopped running.
The clocks all stopped ticking.
The people stopped walking.
The glue all stopped sticking.
The teachers stopped teaching—
Mid-sentence, no less.
The water stopped running—
The sinks are a mess.
The sun didn't set and the moon didn't rise.
The train's in the station.
Not one airplane flies.
And no one can smile, or chuckle, or frown.
And simply because
The computers are down.

Most Monstrous

Frankenstein gives me a fright.
Dracula scares me every night.
Werewolf scarewolf howls his call.
My kid sister scares them all.

Be Polite!

It's always right to be polite,
To get along and never fight.
Don't talk too loud.
Don't walk too proud,
And please don't push
When in a crowd.
So keep your cool.
Don't act too heady—

Shut up and be polite already!

Open-Minded

They told me, "Have an open mind."
I opened up my head.
But all the rain cascaded down
And washed my brain instead.
I hung my wet brain out to dry,
Then put it in my skull.
And though I have no open mind,
I don't mind being dull.

Anna and the Piranhas

Anna stepped into a stream of piranhas.
But she wasn't frightened—
She screamed, ***"Mind your manners!"***

Alphabad

Alpha-bit

ABCDEFG
Skip the middle and
XYZ.

A Dentist Named Phil

There once was a dentist named Phil,
Who would drill, and then drill, and then drill.
When I asked, "Are you done?"
He drilled on, and drilled on,
And he said, "My name's not 'done.' It's Phil."

Doers and Shakers

Some people are doers and shakers.
Some people are shakers and doers.
　　Some make the mistake
　　To befriend a big snake
And leave the world one person fewer.

Young Lady from Linn

There was a young lady from Linn,
Who was so exceedingly thin.
  When she once lost her snack
  In the floorboard's thin crack,
She took off her shoes and jumped in.

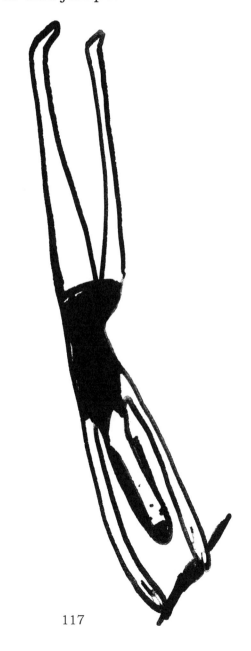

A Young Man from Kalamazoo

A young man from Kalamazoo
Reached a great height of forty foot two.
   With his head in a cloud
   All the thunder's quite loud,
But he certainly savors the view.

A Person Named Pete

There once lived a person named Pete,
Who was so exceedingly neat
    That when it would snow
    On his hands he would go
So he wouldn't get snow on his feet.

Windshield Wipers

Windshield	wipers
Sideways	swipers
Rain	erasers
Snowflake	chasers
Glass	enhancers
Window	dancers

I Hate Flies

I hate flies and I hate fleas.
I hate big fat bumblebees.
I hate nits and I hate gnats.
I hate scary hairy bats.
I hate spiders. I hate slugs.
I hate moths and mealybugs.
I hate termites. I hate ticks.
I hate skinny walking sticks.
I hate ants and I hate mites.
I hate anything that bites!

I Love

I love swifts and I love swans.
I love ducks on sunlit ponds.
I love rabbits. I love hares.
I love cuddly baby bears.
I love martens. I love minks.
I love lions. I love lynx.
I love squirrels. I love snails.
I love dolphins. I love whales.
I love all things big and small.
I love candy best of all.

Tapir Paper

A tapir has a tapered trunk.
Perhaps it is an elephunk.
A tapir's shape is like a horse,
Though shorter and more coarse, of course.
A tapir is a type of rhino—
Without the horn as far as *I* know.

Journey

A journey of one hundred miles
Begins with just one step.
And if your legs
Are nine miles long,
You've got a good start, yep!

Homework Shirk

My hound dog ate my homework.
My kitty chewed it, too.
A taxi ran it over,
And a school bus passing through.
A flood filled it with water.
A cyclone tore it up.
And then my father mixed it
Inside his coffee cup.
Some birds used it for nesting.
They turned it into fuzz.
And that is why my homework
Now looks the way it does.

Zero

Zero is nothing.
Empty and bare.
But when zeros kiss:
Infinity's there.

Eat Feat

My parents always told me that
You are just what you eat.
I ate a sidewalk sandwich and
I turned into a street.
The cars and truck run over me
And big s t r e t c h limousines.
I should have listened to my folks
And eaten all my greens.

Pyramiddle

We started to build this pyramid
Some five hundred years ago.
But though it's so strong,
Something is wrong,
But what, I just
Do not
know
!

Sunset

As the sun is slowly setting on
This beautiful day of December,
I suddenly remember,
My library book was due in November.

My Owl

My owl helps me do my homework.
You know, he's exceedingly wise.
I've got him to actually write it—
He crosses his Ts, dots his Is.
He's filled with incredible knowledge.
Quite often we'll sit and match wits.
My owl helps me doing my homework—
Except when he bites it to bits.

Winter Wear

To go out now
I'd have to wear
My long red flannel underwear,
My three plaid shirts,
My turtleneck sweater
(Especially made for all subzero weather),
My insulated fleece-lined pants
(Imported all the way from France),
My woolen socks,
Warm waterproof shoes,
My a cable-knit scarf
That I rarely use,
My rugged shearling sheepskin hat,
And thermal earmuffs, and not only that,
My arctic parka with sleeves extra-wide—

And that is why I'm staying inside.

Alphabetter

It's time to learn the alphabat.
Oh boy, I mean the alphacat.
Oh, goodness, no, the alphabit.
Uh-oh, that really isn't it.
I must have meant the alphabutt
(By now you must think I'm a nut).
Perhaps it should be alphabees

Oh, let's just learn the ABCs!

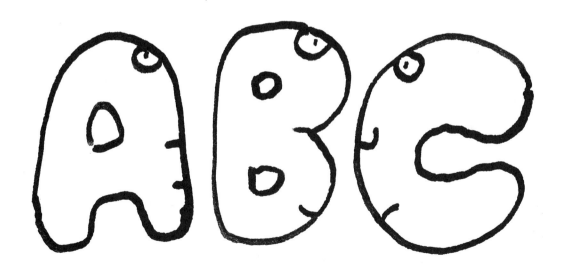

Run Out

Sometimes pens run out of ink.
Sometimes painters run out of pink.
Sometimes eyes run out of blink.
Sometimes brains run out of think.

Caterpillary

A caterpillar's not a cat.
It's not a pillar either.
It turns into a butterfly,
Which isn't butter, neither.

Early to Bed

Early to bed and early to rise
Makes a man healthy, wealthy, and wise.
But late to bed and late to rise
Makes a man lazy with crazy red eyes.

My Mother Has Two Voices

My mother has two voices,
One delicate and dainty.
One loud as an atomic cloud,
So strong it makes you fainty.

When answering the telephone
Her voice is full of mirth,
But how her tone when off the phone
It's heavy as the Earth.

If company should come and call,
Her voice is soft and sweet.
But if we misbehave at all,
It sounds like elephant's feet.

My mother has two voices,
One sweet as baby chicks.
My mother has two voices,
One like a ton of bricks.

Strong Along

My father is strong.
His legs are long.
His arms are made of steel.
And he can lift
A big snowdrift
With one hand
('Snow big deal).
My father is strong.
Strong all along.
Far stronger than my brother.
But though my father's very strong,
He's no match for my mother.

June and December

Although the days of June are long,
And summer sun is very strong,
How quick the month just speeds along.

December has the shortest days.
You barely see the bright sun blaze.
But how the month just stays and stays.

Singsong Wrong

My brother loves to sing a song.
A song he loves to sing.
But when he sings he sings so bad,
It kills birds on the wing.

My brother likes to play guitar.
Guitar he loves to play.
He strums and drums guitar so bad,
The neighbors moved away.

My brother does great magic tricks.
The people gather near.
But when he does his magic tricks
They mostly disappear.

Anna Eats Bananas

Anna ate bananas
She ate at least eleven
Banana-na-na-na-na-na-na-na-na-na-na.

Braces for Faces

Bruno wears braces,
And Hessie and Hector.
Sally's set off the school's metal detector.

Knight Fight

For weeks and weeks Sir Launcelot
Battled with Sir Gawaine
Until it rained so much that they
Both rusted in the rain.

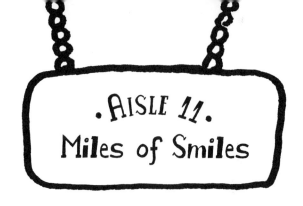

.Aisle 11.
Miles of Smiles

Hand-Me-Downs

Jacob got Joe's hand-me-downs,
Who passed them on to Lou.
When Lou was through,
He gave them to
His second cousin Stu.
When Stu was done,
The clothes passed on.
And now they are all Ned's.
Who gave them to
His dog named Blue
Who tore them into shreds.

Spaceman

I built myself a spaceship,
And I took off in flight.
Within a few short minutes,
I rose a giant height.
I sailed past all the planets,
Then zoomed beyond some star.
I shot out of the galaxy,
A million miles far.
I reached the very end of space.
No farther could I roam.
There wasn't any pizza there
So I returned back home.

BIGFOOT

I searched for BIGFOOT for seventeen years.

I searched for BIGFOOT despite all my fears.

I searched for BIGFOOT through mountains and valleys.

I searched for BIGFOOT

Down back roads and alleys.

I searched for BIGFOOT

In rain, snow, and sleet.

But when I found BIGFOOT

He had stinking feet!

Peter Picked

Peter picked his nose,
Pulled out a garden hose,
A herd of sheep, a flock of geese,
Six chickens who could speak Chinese,
Ten bumblebees, a speeding train,
And NEVER picked his nose again.

I Had a Real Bad Hair Day

I had a Real Bad Hair Day,
Because the weather drizzled.
My hair became all frizzy,
So frazzled and so frizzled.
I had a real bad hair day—
It filled me full of dread,
Until I solved the problem with
A hare upon my head.

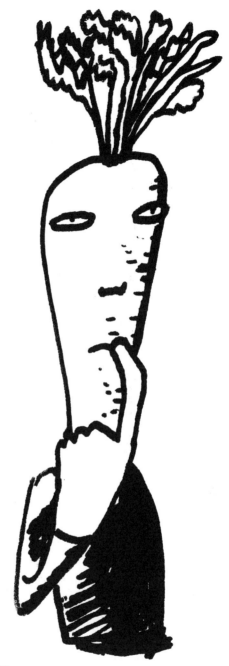

Carrot Head

I ate too many carrots:
One hundred seventeen.
And now I have green hair on top
And skin that's tangerine.

Running Nose

My nose began to run today.
It ran right off my face,
Right past my feet
Into the street
And joined a relay race.
It raced past all the runners,
Before my very eyes.
When all was done,
My nose had won
A ribbon for first prize.

Dreams

I'd like to share with you my dreams,
My wildest fantasies and schemes:
When I grow up one day I plan
To be a famous congressman,
Perhaps even a senator,
Give speeches on the senate floor
Or better yet I'd like to see
My rise up to the presidency

Or maybe run a pharmacy.

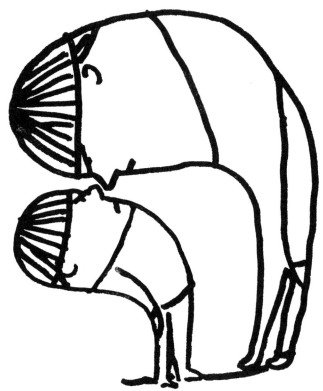

Little

A little pig's a piglet.
A little fish a guppy.
A little cat's a kitten
A little dog a puppy.
A little drip's a drop.
A little cake's a crumb.
My little brother really is
A little bit too dumb.

Advice

Some people search for riches,
While others reach for fame.
Some people change addresses,
And others change their name.
Some look for pleasure traveling,
And others on a shelf.
But my advice for you, my friend,
Is simply be yourself.

It Ain't Over

It ain't over till it's over.
It ain't over till it's through.
It ain't over till you've eaten it—
Or else it's eaten you!

Nothing Lasts Forever

Nothing lasts forever.
All things come and go.
Nothing lasts forever—
Except for weeds, you know.

.Index of. Titles

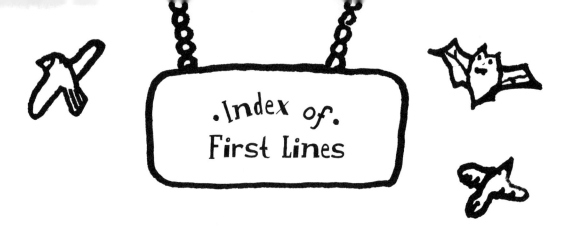

Index of First Lines

Rain, rain—, 90
Rome wasn't built, 65

Snow up to my ankles, 59
Some ladybugs are really men, 4
Some people are doers and
   shakers, 116
Some people search for riches, 147
Some people sit on sofas, 32
Some say the glass is half empty, 50
Sometimes I race a bicycle, 10
Sometimes pens run out of ink, 130

Ten of my brothers are ditty, 81
The big fish eat the small fish, 85
The computers are down, 111
The greatest invention was not
   the car, 96
The mammoths were mammoth
   in size, 99
The rooster crowed this morning, 2
The summer trees are dressed
   in green, 41
The worst book of all, 5
There is no cash in cashews, 92
There lived a man who blew his
   nose, 66
There once lived a person named
   Pete, 119
There once was a dentist named
   Phil, 115
There're 99 people inside of this
   bus, 40
There was a young lady from Linn, 117
There was an old woman, 38
There's not a single cloud today, 33
They call me Slippery, 22
They questioned Abe Lincoln, 44
They said, "Hold your horses!", 93
They say that if, 30

They told me I should call a head, 65
They told me, "Have an open
   mind.", 113
They told the magician, 102
They took an X-ray of my head, 86
This chair is so comfy, 63
Th s po m is mis ing le ters, 28
To go out now, 128
Today I have no appetite, 17
Today my head is in a fog, 72

Water, water everywhere, 52
We have six dogs and seven cats, 23
We started to build this pyramid, 126
We're taking a train to nowhere, 13
Welcome to Poem Depot, 1
What does a, 83
Wild Willy wrestled bears, 64
Windshield wipers, 120
With warty skin and big bug eyes, 98

You can't see time, 99

Zero is nothing, 125

154